Tip of my Tongue

poetry by
LaJenine T. Wilson

edited by
Kathy Foreso

cover art by
LaJenine T. Wilson

iUniverse, Inc.
New York Bloomington

Tip of my Tongue

poetry by LaJenine T. Wilson

iUniverse books may be ordered through booksellers or by contacting:

iUniverse
1663 Liberty Drive
Bloomington, IN 47403
www.iuniverse.com
1-800-Authors (1-800-288-4677)

ISBN: 978-1-4401-1048-1 (pbk)
ISBN: 978-1-4401-1049-8 (ebk)

Printed in the United States of America

iUniverse rev. date: 12/09/2008

for Keyon
the new man
in my life

for Joy Patterson
not your ordinary angel

& for my grandmother
Etta Lee Wilson
a staunch supporter
of the brothas

On the Menu
squad appreciation

PART 1: APPETIZERS
fried chicken & fine black men

PART 2: The MEAT
oh yeah, it's feeding time

PART 3: and for DESSERT
stick out your tongue

squad appreciation

I can't lie. I abandoned this project several times. But some people, and you know who you are, wouldn't leave it alone. So before you sit down to my table, I gotta thank EVERYONE on my squad who got behind me, stayed on my case, got on my freakin nerves and refused to let me quit.

But first, I have to thank GOD for this amazing talent. Until I accepted YOUR purpose for my life, I was just breathing. Then I wanna thank Bea Wilson, the mother of all mothers and my grandmother, Etta Lee Wilson, who made me laugh without even trying. *Thanks a lot.*

To my entire family. From my Aunt Gloria to my Uncle Felton, from my cousin Ashleigh to my Aunt Elestine. Thanks for the love, the support and the encouragement even when you didn't understand what I was trying to say. To Willie, who made sure my belly and my pockets were full. Margaret Douglas, who served me my first cup of coffee, a little cream and way too much sugar. The Russell Family, the Fambro Family and the Williams Family.

To my squad. Aria Nicole, who beat me to the finish line. Hazel Fambro, for being there through allllllllllllllll the drama. Cartresia Hudson, my loud Leo sista. Lisa Whitehead, my therapist in training and Carolyn Ivey, my homegirl.

To my good friend, Gregory Beatty, for always giving it to me straight. Keeping it Real 101 should be a prerequisite for us all. Zellie Orr for insisting that I write. Joyce (where is my fried corn), Anethia, Michelle (where is my tomato pie), Charisa (where is my corn beef hash), Shanna, Felecia (a.k.a. Poohgina), Dawn, Shatisha, Marylou (my prayer partner) & Deion for making my time in the corporate arena a little less painful. DAMN, the things we do for hot water. My EPA family: Ro, Ann, Lashon, Darryl, Larry, Brenita, Bridget and Carolyn for having pity on this little girl from Georgia State.

To my pastor, Dr. William E. Flippin, Sr., for your leadership and members of Greater Piney Grove, especially Ms. Barbara Williams for reminding me that I had a voice and Mrs. Bernstine Hollis, who said I would survive. You were right Mrs. Hollis. I will.

To my English teachers/instructors, from Southside Comprehensive High School to Georgia State, who saw meaning and purpose in my scribble. Angela Robinson, Marquise Jackson & Vickie Whitlock for supporting me as I moved from production assistant to senior producer of the always fabulous IN CONTACT. The editors and staff at the Atlanta Tribune & The Times in Gainesville for giving me and my journalistic aspirations a chance, even when I didn't.

To Cecelia, Clint, Janice, Philisia & Kim at Lestyles in Decatur for keeping every hair in place and staying on my case until I got this thing done.

To Kathy Foreso for lending your eyes to this project and Renee with N'DigoDesign for being the best at what you do.

To Stefen Micko and Theresa Davis (two of the best Atlanta has to offer), for welcoming me back to the spoken word scene and Mocha Match Cafe. To black girl poets across the country struggling to find the right words. Trust me. They will come. To Nikki Giovanni, one of the greatest poets that ever lived, for opening my eyes to this thing called poetry (po-eh- tree). To Jessica Care Moore, for not only being a gifted writer/ poet but for also being a sharp businesswoman. I need and greatly appreciate your example. And to Jill Scott, proof that real talent still exists. But as you probably already know, the world just ain't ready.

I'll take my chances.

Love,
La

this is not a poem, but DAMN…
I been wanting to say this a long time…

Tip of my Tongue

PART 1: APPETIZERS
fried chicken & fine black men

*my sister Bay

legs closed, eyes open
grandma praying
mama hoping
hoping I don't end up like my sister Bay

skirts short and tight, lips glossy red
old men stared in disbelief
old women shook their heads
they ran to their porches to see
when Bay walked down the street

five kids by three different men
a night at the club
she'd be in love again
the next day she'd give it up to a man
without knowing his last name

busted lips, swollen eyes
her new man beat her down
enjoyed her cries
then promised not to ever raise his fist
to her face again

legs open, eyes closed
dried up blood left a trail from her nose
though her face was badly scarred
we knew the naked body was my sister Bay

*fine black man

deep in my soul lives a woman full of hate
sick of being torn down tired of having to wait
for the man of her dreams to walk into her life
I didn't know the brotha had five kids
he failed to mention he had a wife

I guess I should've known something was wrong
when he told me he didn't have a phone
or as soon as renovations were complete
he would invite me to his home

I knew I couldn't have this man to myself
but I went along with the brotha's game
jumping like he was Denzel or somebody
every time he remembered my name

girl this brotha was so fine
I never looked in brown eyes so deep
his kisses made me want to get undressed
I never tasted a brotha so sweet

mama told me when I was a little girl
I should always have a plan
I didn't know it required a special technique
to love a fine black man

*fried chicken

I laid out some chicken to fry after church
I sent my boy at some okra and peas
fried chicken ain't nothing without collard greens
or some macaroni and cheese
I been told that it's greasy and fattening
Dr. Jones said it's bad for my health
but what do he know about good eating
and what do I care about death

*black brand man

up one aisle
then down another
I push
my cart
searching for
the right brand
of man
not the all-AMERICAN brand
in the red WHITE
and blue box
but a flavorful one
I tried some of the
other brands
but they always let me down
two hours after having
an Asian experience
I was hungry again
the Puerto Rican special
though visually and physically filling
came with too many friends
there was one that didn't know
where to put it
another one didn't have enough
to put
but the brotha I had last week
was nice
yeah
that brotha
was alright

*between me & the moon

I can't sleep tonight
with constant thoughts of being loved
stuck in my head
keeping me awake
I stare up at the ceiling
listen to night sounds go by
as I chat with the moon
who on this particular night
is so fed up
with my conversation
he insists
that I be quiet
and go to sleep

*understanding of what don't rhyme

I was happy to hear that rhyming
was not required
moon june tune
sounds good
but don't make sense together
like we need to figure some things out
before we die
searching to find the right word
that rhymes with self-destruction
while making sense
is too hard
so we don't read
what don't rhyme
for understanding

*funky days

everyone wants to know
when I'll do something new
like it's that easy
in the funk I'm in
to pull something original
out my butt
sometimes bad moods don't end in rhyming
sometimes being new ain't always good
though my thoughts are infinite
and my ideas just as great
funk tends to stifle creativity
still I guess I should be happy
they expect something new
even on funky days

*cool ass white girl

she was my cousin
I never told nobody
but she was
and except for that chain
hanging from her ear to her nose
she was a cool ass white girl
she liked to get high
I liked to get high
so we clicked
she took me to get my first tattoo
I took her to hear some black poets
she let me borrow her Aerosmith cd
so I introduced her to the realness of Tupac
she said she wouldn't mind doing him
if she could do a black man
I said it's too late
we already killed him
she said damn
that's too bad

*due to heavy breathing

like an infectious disease
mr. executive vice-president in charge of
getting his freak on
sought to get his freak on
several times a week
I voiced my concerns
in regards to his inappropriate behavior
but boss man didn't seem to hear me
or due to heavy breathing
I was being ignored
cause when he slid his hand
inside my blouse
and squeezed my breast
the only response I got from him was
I'd better get use to his lovin'
if I planned on keeping my job

*pebbles

I thought I had to go real bad
so I ran to the bathroom
with my Ebony
contracting back
and forth
anticipating a big one
cause I had tacos and burritos for lunch
using stomach muscles
thigh muscles
straining
grunting
waiting
for this big plop
followed by the inevitable splash
but instead all I heard was a tiny pebble
that's when I looked at my Ebony
in aggravation
thinking
I know
that ain't all

*knee high grass

up to my knees
some up to my thighs
reaching for my behind
but I stomp through it
looking for a stupid ball
wondering why my uncle didn't cut the grass
like grandma said
I would turn around
go back in the house
it ain't like they want girls to play no way
but I keep looking
cause everybody waiting on me
to come back
and since I picked center field
or maybe it picked me
I keep going
huffing
puffing
itching
cussing
looking for a stupid ball
I can't even hit

*nice white sheets

I might
melt
if he
holds me
too tight
and spread
my love
all over
his nice
white sheets

*whatever

he could breathe on me
sweat if he wanted to
something that fine
I probably wouldn't mine
if he stared a hole between my breasts
or left indentations between my thighs
I'd just drive myself to the doctor
and tell him
I was permissively attacked
by a brotha
too fine
to be accused
of any wrongdoing

*hungry

I am not
as hungry
as I seem
despite
what daddy thinks
and mama says
I have reasons
some valid
for wanting
and trying
to have
them all

*I called him nice

he said his name
was Marco
but I called him nice
a soothing image
to hold in my thoughts
and press against my soul
something good to look at
when everything
and everyone else
in my world
looks the same
my eyes go
on the hunt
for some magnificent views
just like
this one
with smooth
dark skin
and hypnotic brown eyes
that make a sister wish
she was this fortunate
everyday

*just like on t.v.

if I move with you
can we eat dinner
at the same time
just like they do on t.v.
can we sit down at the table
and talk about what we did all day
clean the kitchen together
I wash
you dry
watch the evening news
share our views
on the president's decision
if I move with you
will you bring me flowers for no reason
just like they do on t.v.
kiss my cheek when you enter the room
rub my back on your way out
and sometimes can we lie in bed
and hold each other
without you trying to stick yourself
in me

*bus to macon

four
five times
a year
you come
toting coconut cake
and barbecue sandwiches
like you forgot I'm allergic to coconut
and I don't eat meat
I say come in mama
take off your coat
you say alright
we sit down
you smile
I smile
you say how you been
I say I been fine
you say how's your husband
I say he's been fine
you say that's good
I sigh
you smile
I look away
you smile some more
I ask about Aunt Mattie's hip
but what I really wanna know is
how long
are you planning
to stay

PART 2: The MEAT
oh yeah, it's feeding time

*come on in

welcome to America
land of the free to take
as many lives as you can
then say you was insane
home of small-minded punks
with guns
position takers
aspiring players
sick-in-the-head priests
shady ass police
misplaced dreams
get-rich-quick schemes
drug dealers
baby killers
welcome to America
where we'll uphold
and protect your freedom
while you plot to destroy
our sense of security
then lay back and chill
while you plan your next attack
come on in

*feeding time

during our designated month
we are fed bits of
Martin and Malcolm
Harriet and Rosa
Frederick and Charles
told how wonderful it is to be black
how proud we should feel
how fortunate we are to be the children
of slaves doctors writers lawyers
civic leaders who led this great nation
to this great state
of freedom
told how wonderful it is to be alive
and black
in America
then on March 1st
when feeding time is over
our stomachs start to growl
like we hadn't just been fed
28 (or 29) days worth of
black history

*issues

the sign said
all poets welcomed
but should've said
all poets welcomed
long as you ain't
angry
black
pissed at the government
and still tripping off
that inequality shit
if you have love poems
come in
if you're armed
with issues
stay the fuck out
no killing poems
no anti-Bush poems
no affirmative-action poems
no we still trying to overcome poems
no white man holding me down
white women taking all our good men poems
no drive-by poems
no issues
just love
no issues
just love
love
love

*ain't no punk

our last president
was a freak
but his daughter wasn't a drunk
and his wife
didn't need permission
to speak her mind
but you ain't no punk
mr. president
cause you was bold enough
to send our troops
to hunt for a lunatic
        more arrogant than yourself
and it takes guts
to make impelling speeches
from the white house lawn
did Colin tell you to say that
did Condoleezza tell you to say that
did your daddy tell you to say that
or did you grow that brain all by yo self
your approval rating
shot up mr. president
with a boost to national morale
now what you gonna do about this sagging economy

*free

how free is free
when I got spies
with digital eyes
watching me
trying to see inside me
trying to get inside my head
infiltrating my bedroom
lurking under my bed
they swear I got something to hide
since I lied about where I been
and refused to stay hemmed in
my designated spot
now I can't be trusted
now they seem disgusted
with my frequent attempts
to privatize my own life
every since www.tellallmydamnbusiness
told all my damn business
I been seen around town in disguise
by the same set of digital eyes
I caught looking between my thighs
I don't stand by the window at night
afraid the beams from their infrared lights
will expose the little privacy I got left
leave me wondering if
this pain in my chest
and this inability to rest
will ever subside
cause if I sneeze right now
they'll know
and try to make it so
I can't blow my nose
without permission
can't have an orgasm
without submitting to some tests

trying to find out what drugs I'm on
without testing my pee
invading me
trying to see which freak
I let get in me tonight
they say I'm free
but that ain't right
I was never told
but I feel like I been sold
and right now I'm in some consumer's bag
waiting to be had
by some over inquisitive mind
wanting to know
if my father's white
if I ever think about naked women
where I was last Friday night
if I was spending time with my lesbian friends
performing sexual acts for nameless men
am I secretly an undercover ho
hunching chairs
swinging round poles
they wanna know
they say I'm free
but I can't tell

*if I fuck the president

if I fuck the president
would that make me a political ho
entitled to all the perks
afforded political hoes

if I fuck the president
would he start calling me every night
saying how the first lady's tripping
begging me to talk dirty
telling me his freaky dreams
describing how he wants to do it
next time we're alone

if I fuck the president
then can I sit down with barbara walters
give her the blow by blow
write a book about my painful experience
then hobnob with Julia Roberts and Brad Pitt
like fucking and sucking the president
deserves an award

if I fuck the president good
will secret service agents come after me
and try to charge me
with turning the president out

*chocolate milk confusion

here I go again
trying to be a poet
wrapping you all up in
some more nonsense
taking you
twisting you
thoroughly confusing you
making you wonder what I meant
when I said I don't want to
did I mean make love or be alone
have you searching for symbolism
in chocolate milk
looking for significance
in eggs with no cheese
have you begging
baby
please
    please
        please
don't write no more
don't rhyme no more
don't talk no more
it's too confusing
what did you mean
when you said white
did you mean yellow
red orange green
what did you mean
is the sky really blue
is the water really wet
is the...
    is the...
        is the...

have you asking
why
        why
                why
do you do this to me
why did you say good-night
then begin to undress
is it really good
is it really night
I don't know what you mean
I don't knowwwwwwwwwwwwwwwwwwwwwww

*call me super

your eyes light up
when I enter the room
something inside you moves
conversation ends
a list of possibilities
begins to emerge
graced with Beverly cheeks
Naomi lips
Iman eyes
and Tyra hips
I got you thinking of ways to make me smile
whisper in my ear baby
c'mon tell me
 I'm the one
tomorrow fly me to New York
introduce me to your colleagues
set me up in a five-star hotel
while you devise ways to cover my imperfections
conceal my infidelities
schedule me for an impromptu class
on how to walk
and how to sit
how to breathe
how to shit
stick me in a Versace gown
do something crazy with my hair
pluck me
squeeze me
brush me
spray me
dip my skinny ass in foundation
and call me
super

*1-800-GET-SOME
(why I stay broke)

an unforeseen number
of junkies
on the planet
all dialing at the same time
bum rushing the toll free lines
for some new and improved shit
a blue-eyed pusher is on my t.v.
yelling for me
to dial 1-800-GET-SOME
he keep saying
dial 1-800-GET-SOME
and I will
but I won't
and still missing
is the mental and emotional ability
I need to resist
Ms. COACH
and Ms. GUCCI
see that's why I stay broke
that's why
I stay
broke
cause my shoes
MUST match my purse
MUST match my belt
MUST match my empty
bank account
I seriously
doubt
MR. SOCIAL SECURITY
will consider me
an exception
when I'm wrinkled
and gray

after years
of providing exceptional   SIRRRRRvice
and constantly proving my   LO   YAL   TY
my government
will take one look
at me and say
you need
WHAT?????

*brown pill

the purple pill is for my head
the green pill keeps my belly from swelling
the red pill suppose to give me energy
the blue one suppose to ease my cramps
the white one is still on the counter
          since I often question its effectiveness
but the brown one
well
you just make me feel good all over

*addicted

I'm the fiend
in the alley giving blow jobs
for a dime bag of him
nothing matters to me no more
I don't care who sees
my desperation
when I'm strung out
tripping
addicted
to this new drug
called my man
my pcp
my ecstasy
my cocaine
I smoke him when I want to feel real good
I split him out into neat little rows
then inhale
each line of him
nice
and slow
he turns my eyes red
and my lips white
he's got me feeling like
something's crawling up my neck
I hear voices pouring out my head
sometimes I see faces
that ain't even there
but I don't care
shit
I'm not scared
of the long-term effects
long as he keeps moving through my veins
numbing all traces
of pain
long as he keeps

loving me
like this
I won't seek professional help
cause I'm addicted
and he's
the dope
that keeps me

*another serving of you

I stand in line
with my bowl
and my spoon
waiting for another serving
of you
but Tameka
Sheena
Nakia
and Rene
have been in line
since 5 a.m.
and judging from the sounds
coming from their stomachs
I doubt
they'll let me
cut in line

*on an elevator
(for the good smelling brothas I love)

the scent
of his cologne
tampered with
my thinking
so I was forced to stop thinking
            logical thoughts
and imagine what he'd
smell like in the dark
or on an elevator
or on a dark elevator
or on a dark elevator stuck between floors
way
up
high
would he smell the same
would he be this intoxicating
if
we
were
alone?

*a no show

it felt good
so I stayed
all weekend
and prayed
Monday morning would be
a no show
but she did show
early
bright
noisy as hell
breaking the spells
he'd cast on me
breaking the spells
I'd cast on him
disrupting the mood
that only Friday night
could bring

*yesterday

it was cold
and wet
and hot
all at once
and I could not see
through the cloud of bullshit
coming from your mouth
but could hear very well
when you said
good-bye baby
I can't make no more
commitments
and being that I'd just
fixed your plate
I
was
pissed

*he musta forgot

I overheard him tell one of his boys
he don't know
how I'll make it
after he's gone
he musta forgot
his broke ass moved in
with me

*huh, baby

if I apologize
for having views
will you love me
like you use to
if I submit
stop acting like the bitch
you say I've become
from overexposure
to the truth
can I speak my mind
sometimes
huh, baby
can I speak my mind
if I promise not to disagree
in public
not insist that you compromise
eat all my fried lies
at dinnertime
will you be my man again
huh, baby
will you be my man
again

*missing

someone stole my man
while I was sleep
and brought me a freak
in his place
the last few nights
I been having dinner with
this confused brotha
who looks like my man
even smells like my man
but sounds nothing like my man
when he opens his mouth
cause instead of telling me
how much he loves me
dude says he's no longer able
to sustain me
too busy trying to be me
too busy plotting ways
to steal my breasts and my hips
probably wants my eyes
and my lips too
busy searching for femininity
under a skirt he stole from me
I tried filing a missing person's report
see if they could possibly
put out an a.p.b.
but authorities
keeping telling me
to give him more time
he ain't been gone
long enough
ma'am
give him
more time

*can't breathe

open my eyes
      I see your face
thinking I'll be slick
and escape
but when I close my eyes
      I see your face
in my coffee
      I see your face
on the t.v. screen
      I see your face
even up in the sky
      I see your face
      I see your face
      I see your face
everywhere
all I'm trying to say is
damn baby
I
can't
breathe

*I ain't forgot

I heard you screaming my name
from the street below
demanding I open the door
so you could get your things
but the last time
you demanded
and I complied
good shit got broken
feelings got hurt
and I called off work three days
scared you'd come back
and shoot my brains out
like you said
I ain't
forgot

*hungry 2
(for me and for Hazel)

hungry
I was the fool
chasing two-piece snacks
when what my mind
and body
really wanted
was a meal
served with ALLLLLLLLLLLLLLLLLLLLLLLL
the trimmings
i.e. a fine brotha
deluxe
and I do mean
DDDDDDDDDDDDDDDDDDDDDDDDELUXE

*no love
(for Cecelia)

I checked the shelves for it
but could find it stacked nowhere
so I asked the hateful heifer behind the desk
where they kept it
and she said ain't no love here
then I asked if they'd be getting some in
and she said ain't no love here
then I asked if she knew who else carried it
and she said ain't no love here
so I left
disappointed
cause I promised Cecelia
I'd write more loving caring poems
now she'll have to keep reading
that dark crap
she don't like

*confiscated...I'm missing...the video...

confiscated items
were placed
in the box
I was told
to check there
if I'd recently
lost my
mind
cause the last time
I saw myself
was right before
I jumped
in his bed
the last time
I heard
my own voice
was right before
he crept in
my head
I been dropping
pieces of me
in my haste to be
some rich MC's ho
afraid the world
won't notice
unless I shake ass
on the video

*loving you

he claims he loves you
and only you
but last night
when he was loving her
was he loving you
last night when he was
whispering in her ear
filling her head
with the same lies
he's telling you
was he loving you
when he was
kissing
and hugging
squeezing
and rubbing on her
was he loving you
later when he climbed in bed
with you
still smelling like
what he'd done with her
was he loving you
are you loving you
when you pretend
not to notice
the stench

*two days

I cram my life
in two days
cause during the other five
I'm on master's time
and my mind
ain't my mind
and my actions
ain't my actions
just some approved reactions
to someone's dissatisfaction
with the way I perform my j - o - b
or the way I fulfill
my po-si-tion
from nine to five
I'm whoever
doing whatever
boss lady says
for that check
come Friday night
I let go
cause Monday morning I know
I got four more days
till I see me again

*last night at the spot

last night
me and my girls went to the spot
to hear some black poets
speak on being black
staying black
and getting blacker
in 2002
then I saw you
up on stage
a young
intelligent brotha
with something more to say
than hey bitch
while grabbing your dick
sipping on strawberry daiquiris
filling up on triple hot wings
watching you do your thing
my whole table was grasping the message
feeling the flow
but I wanted to know
if later
you could love me to sleep
with your intellect

*hostage

I'm being held hostage
by closet pimps and undercover hoes
who don't want their freaky habits exposed
to the public
they was feeling me at first
they said they loved my flow
I guess as long as my flow
didn't step on toes
or damage wealthy egos
now they got me held up
in a cramped room
with no windows
five minutes ago they was with it
now they demanding that I change it
pretend not to see what I see
not to hear what I hear
late at night on my street
dodging bullets
trying to survive
in air thick with death
while guards monitor the premises
of their palatial estates
I sleep in abandoned buildings
cover up with cardboard boxes
turn tricks just so I can eat
but in my efforts
to get back on my feet
I can't even say
what I wanna say
since they insist freedom of speech
is only free to those
who can afford it
I am still subject
to butterfly quotas
required to give a damn

about green grass
and blue skies
waterfalls
and butterflies
they need
more pretty
from a past littered
with nothing
but ugly
they need
more pretty

*enough
(for my 10+ years in the corporate arena...I tried and
I tried, but I never loved you)

I puffed on you
long enough
inhaled you in
blew you out
inhaled you in
blew you out
so many times
I lost count around
one-hundred
forty-six thousand
eight-hundred
twenty-three
see we never really
got along that well
but hell I tried
since you were
so damn comfortable
even made it possible
for me to get my stuff checked
and my teeth cleaned
regularly
unfortunately
there comes a time
when we must
attempt to escape
unhealthy habits
and you
my nine
to five
are no exception

*these words are all I got

these words are all I got
and like roaches
they trying to take them too
they already invaded
my privacy
now they after my thoughts
replacing every other word
rearranging every other line
changing my t's
to d's
and my q's
to u's
then conveniently
misplacing
what I need to spell
K_SS MY BL_CK _SS
since their involvement
my purpose has drastically changed
since they keep tampering with my brain
I ain't the same person
I mean I look like me
and sound like me
but I feel like somebody else
trying to fill a void
that ain't even mine
while my words
get twisted
out of shape
to create
new meaning
unwanted effects
and more confusion
up on stage
trying to hold it together

as I babble
and digress
from my original intent
I hope this audience
can make sense
out of nonsense

PART 3: and for DESSERT
stick out your tongue

*the afterglow

feeling especially
energetic
this morning
I open my blinds
to ms. sunshine
select track three on my jill scott cd
plug in my mr. coffee maker
scramble two eggs
grate some cheese
fry some bacon
almost burn some toast
peel two apples
and squeeze some juice
the whole time
smiling and humming
smiling and humming
like it's the 1st
or the 15th
like I got the entire day off   wit pay
like the afterglow
causing my morning delusions
won't eventually
wear off

*ransacked

you broke in once before
ransacked my entire life
      cracked open my head
      turned over my mind
      pried open my chest
      yanked out my heart
      left my feelings for you
      scattered
      everywhere
but unlike other
potential suspects

you didn't run

from the mess

that you made

*when you touch me

I melt like
fresh butter
in a hot skillet
or a chocolate bar
trapped in a parked car
in the summer time
when you
touch
me

*thirsty

I am
still
thirsty
even though
you've been
quite generous
when pouring
your love
on me
I still
want
you

*say when

I was
no good
so weak
I melted
time he said
hello
right there
on another
crazy busy sidewalk
to the expected delight
of his boys
to the damn shame
of my girls
I went from
strong black woman
I don't need
no man
to sustain me
to say when baby
just
say
when

*the way it feels

you say
you like the way
it feels
when I'm on top
gazing down
into your
high
brown eyes
>   quietly communicating
>   my intense love
>   for you
>   and this sport
I say
I like the way
it feels
>   period

*I do

I heard she
had one
so I wanted one too
and the big fat
diamond ring
that screams
someone actually
wanted my needy behind
and the lavish wedding
and the loveless marriage
that follows
but precedes
the messy divorce
and the two bullets
in my head
when husband finds out
I went out
and got myself
a new man
right before he pulled
the trigger
he said trick
remember when
you said
I *do*
I said
I *do*
I *do*
but I really
didn't

*hindsight

you wanna
back back now
take it all back now
you be the man
you shoulda been
me be the woman
I coulda been
before when you weren't
rotting in the trunk
of your beloved Cadillac
and I wasn't covered
in type O blood
blood

oh how romantic
oh how
sweet
just me   no you
and your 22
just me   no you
and your 22

*if you must shoot

in my country
where it is customary
to shoot first
and ask questions
later
that brotha
shot
first
so later
after tending superficial wounds
injuries sustained while being grazed
by one tragically overused
hey baby
let me holla at you a minute
I wanted to know
did I say my name
was *baby*
and if you must shoot
must you use
antiquated lines
as your
ammunition

*big legs

he say he loves
my big legs
and my big behind
but my big mind
and my big dreams
          and the resulting chatter
often get on his nerves
last week
he asked if I could
hold it down a little
I was like my big mind
or my big dreams
that fool said
BOTH

*stick out your tongue

what's left of
my first pay check
in hand
I asked the lady
with the silver dreads
if she'd pierce my tongue
she said
hell nahhhhhhhhhhhh
I ain't no murderer
I run a respectable business here
respectable
yeah okay respectable
    did I forget to mention that big ass
    SATIN LIVES tattoo
so I said
I got thirty
she said
you young people
got life confused
I said
how about forty
she said
young asses
always trying to band-aid bullet wounds
I said
alright fifty
and that's it
I'm out
she said
stick out your tongue baby
stick out
your tongue

*sounds like shacking
(for Etta)

I knew grandma
would not approve
of my shacking
but like I tried to explain
two single people
living in the same house
sleeping in the same bed
occasionally sharing
the same meal
with intentions to someday
be married
ain't the same thing

she said
oh really

*silly

this one old dude
looked at me
and asked
what kinda poet
you s'pose to be
he said
you too cute
I said ohhhhhhhhhhhhhhhhhh
all poets are tore up
is that what you saying
he said
no, but they need to know
something besides
their name
you don't look like
you know shit
I said
I know I ain't having
this silly conversation
he said
that's a start

*deep end

his kisses
dared me
to jump
so I jumped
in the deep end
of his love
where I swam
like my summer
was ending

*breathe

this morning
his love for me
extended all the way
into the kitchen
where he
buttered my toast
and extra cheesed my grits
just the way I like
per   fect   ly
later we resumed
what I assumed
was over
        for the day
then he pleasantly surprise me
exerting extra energy
to tackle my list
        baby please mow the…
        sweetie please trim the…
        honey please wash the…
all before dinner
which he made too
and all I had to do
was breathe

*fresh-picked mama
(for Bea, my mama)

in this third
and final pot
of self-expression
I promise only
the freshest
ingredients
so floating amongst
my greens
and peas
you will find
no punks
or pimps
posing
as presidents
or fine
black
men
but then as me
and my pen
hustle towards
other savory
possibilities
on our way
to the last page
in this freakin book
I can't help
but be tempted
by the aroma of
finally figuring
some shit out
life is too short
not to try
life is too short
not to try

so I tried
and some of you liked
and that was good enough
for me
but see
there are some
greedy motherfuckers
in the world
who'll only want
more
more
more
unfortunately
there will be
no more servings
of bad relationships
crack addiction
or fried chicken
I won't even bother
telling you
about my mama *(though she was fresh picked)*
and all the crazy things
she says
about love

*Jill
(for Jill Scott and real talent)

this last one
is for Jill Scott
a naturally creative
lyrically innovative sistah
who while living her life
like it's golden
still failed to work
hard enough
for in this land
of ass shakers
I haven't seen her
shake it
one time

*my new name
(for Keyon)

that first evening
I saw you
I knew
mommy would be
my new name
unlike all the other names
I'd been given
by brothas in my past
some sexy
        some silly
                some sweet
mommy would be
the most important
one of all
for the rest of my life
        or until puberty strikes
then I'm just plain ma